Praise for
Abuela Lore

"In Abuela Lore, Isabella Santana speaks to us in a poetic voice that is both powerfully new and startlingly familiar. Santana reaffirms how we all come to know the divine feminine—through flesh and blood women who have lived and suffered and learned, "la voz de mi abuela/será mi guia," yet Yolis and Chica are not in any way reduced to their roles as grandmothers or idealized archetypes. The concluding poems leave us knowing that the belief and example of real women is what is needed to begin to navigate the world as both a woman and a poet."

—ire'ne lara silva,
2023 Texas State Poet Laureate

"Epic and elegant in its simplicity. Each poem in Abuela Lore is a mystical landscape. Las abuelas, Chica y Yolis, are mythic in proportion and breathtakingly beautiful. Isabella Santana is a powerful fresh voice from the lands of las Americas/Turtle Island/Abya Yala. The words of her pen; much like the volcano of Tungurahua, Ecuador and the movement of the 1976 Terremoto in Guatemala; spit fire and shift earth. A pristine collection that flows on the diaspora con las mariposas. This poet is one to watch and I'm so blessed to encounter her medicine so early in her writing career."

—Brenda Vaca,
Writer and Publisher, Riot of Roses Publishing House

"Embark on a stirring literary journey with Isabella Santana, a young poet whose collection, Abuela Lore, is a poignant love letter to the abuelas shaping her essence. As a first-generation Latina, Isabella skillfully weaves the narratives of Mami Yolis and Chica, inviting readers into the heart of a familiar theme for many first-gen Latinas. Abuela Lore explores the overlapping of shared identities, offering a concise and powerful introduction to Latino culture. This collection is a poetic homage and a testament to the resilience in familial bonds, celebrating the strength of our grandmothers and the women who shape our narratives."

—Fernanda Kelly
Emmy Award-winning Television Hos

"Abuela Lore is a vivid collection of poems that weaves together memory, grief, ancestral reverence and the depths of a grandmother's love in beautiful, surprising and truth-telling ways. In this two-part chapbook, Isabella Santana, compels us to bear witness to the magical, and deeply human, experience of grandmothering-- inviting us to step closer into the intricate identities folded in between girl and grandmother. Her words are rooted in love. And they come together to convey a veneration of her elders--their beauties and strengths--while reckoning with their imperfections and utter human-ness with curiosity, grace and compassion."

—Daad Sharfi
Poet. Immigration attorney

"Abuela Lore is a must read for all of us that forever carry our abuelas deep inside our heart. The power, pain, laughs and endless love found in each word shook me to the core, touching my soul profoundly, awakening hidden emotions, and unlocking the unconditional love that lives within us...the kind of love that only an abuela can give. The poems in Abuela Lore not only resonate deeply; this masterpiece also invites us to remember, reconcile and reflect on the impact that our abuelas stories continue to have in our lives, standing the test of time and surviving future generations to come."

— Argelia Atilano
Radio & TV Broadcaster

"Raw. Magical. Resistant! Beautifully haunting throughout, while embodying the healing and tender spirit of a culture and the dedicatory women of Abuela Lore. A full circle raza fairy tale! Abuela Lore takes you on a compelling journey through the lives of two strong and dynamic abuelas (grandmothers), and what a dynamic generational journey it is! Love letter-esque as a whole, yet each poem weaves together interconnected tales of bravery, resistance, and the healing magic that comes from a culture as unique and fearless as Chica and Mami Yolis themselves! Being a LatinX writer is a resistance unto itself, but moreover, Abuela Lore also aligns with the spirit of both a heartrending call to action and the healing remedio (remedy) to injustice. Making space for daring poetic voices is invaluable, and Isabella Santana's bold and magical chapbook Abuela Lore is proof of just that!"

—**Yvonne Acosta**
Poet, WriteGirl Volunteer

Abuela Lore

Abuela Lore
First Edition Copyright © 2024
Published by Somos en escrito Literary Foundation Press,
Berkeley, California
www.somosenescrito.com

Disclaimer: The views, thoughts, and opinions expressed in the text belong solely to the author, and do not necessarily represent those of the Somos en escrito Literary Foundation.

Trademark notice: Product or corporate names may be trademarks or registered trademarks, and are used only for identification and explanation without intent to infringe.

Library of Congress Cataloging-in-Publication Data
A catalog record for this book has been requested
ISBN: 979-8-9902068-1-6

Typeset in Adobe Garamond Pro

The Somos en escrito Literary Foundation is an all Raza-run, independent press that operates Somos en escrito Magazine and Somos en escrito Press, the book publishing unit: a tax-exempt, nonprofit organization, IRS Code number 81-3162209.

For any inquiries, write to Somos en escrito Literary Foundation Press at
somosenescrito@gmail.com

Cover design Isabella Santana & Luz Schweig

Abuela Lore

ISABELLA SANTANA

SOMOS EN ESCRITO
LITERARY FOUNDATION PRESS

BERKELEY
2024

Contents

Uno: Cuento de hadas

Introduction to my abuelas	3
Terremoto	4
Aventura	6
Pastaza Te Lleva	8
Tungurahua	9
When My Abuelas Get Drunk	10
Una Oda A Mi Mami Yolis	12
Ángel	13
You will be number one	15
Ave Maria	18

Dos: Las mujeres májicas Tambien sufren

No take backs	23
First gen	24
Chica doesn't smile in photos	26
Chica's bedtime song	27
The lemon picking thief	28
Ana Dominga is dead	30
Yolis, did you know?	33
Sana sana	35
Mi Mami Yolis the free woman	37
Good Girl	40
Manuela Monzón de Mendoza, the poet	42
Notes	45
Acknowledgements	49
About the Author	51

Uno:

Cuentos de hadas

YOLIS (LEFT) CHICA (RIGHT)
February, 2020

Introduction to my Abuelas

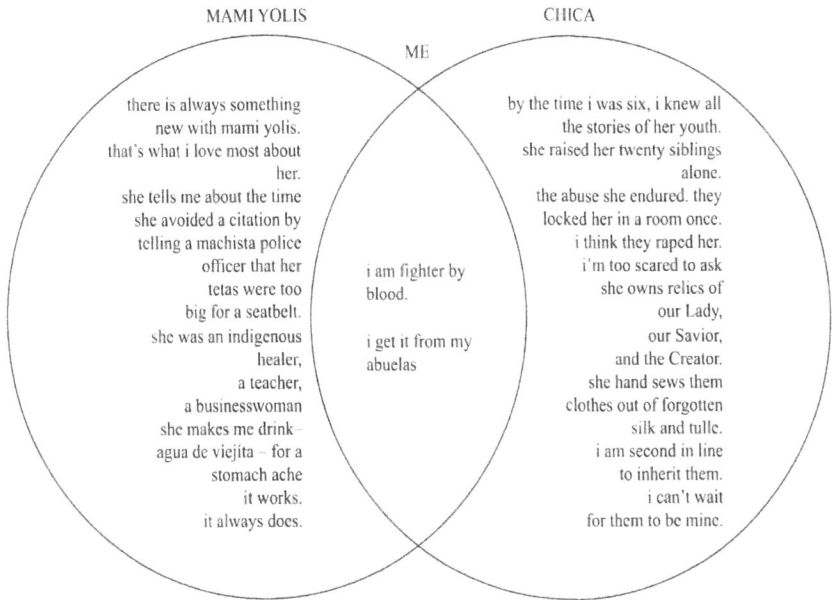

MAMI YOLIS

CHICA

ME

there is always something
new with mami yolis.
that's what i love most about
her.
she tells me about the time
she avoided a citation by
telling a machista police
officer that her
tetas were too
big for a seatbelt.
she was an indigenous
healer,
a teacher,
a businesswoman
she makes me drink–
agua de viejita – for a
stomach ache
it works.
it always does.

i am fighter by
blood.

i get it from my
abuelas

by the time i was six, i knew all
the stories of her youth.
she raised her twenty siblings
alone.
the abuse she endured. they
locked her in a room once.
i think they raped her.
i'm too scared to ask
she owns relics of
our Lady,
our Savior,
and the Creator.
she hand sews them
clothes out of forgotten
silk and tulle.
i am second in line
to inherit them.
i can't wait
for them to be mine.

Terremoto

Chica tells me that the first time the world crumbled was the morning of the
terremoto

             (a note: not a temblor, a terremoto. they are
    different).
She watched her house buckle, the walls wiggling as they caved in.
The Earth swallowed up the bakery where she got pan dulce
devouring all the bread and bakers in one suffocating gulp.
             (The aftershocks, a power only granted to Nuestro
    Dios,
              destroyed churches and monasteries built en el
    Nombre de Dios)

I bet that the second time Chica's
world crumbled was when she came to America.
culture shock brought her to her knees. Every step
shifting the San Andreas, dragging her into its molten factories
eroded her, cracking her into pieces that would eventually become a mosaic
a fractured self

    Run:
watch the world dissolve into granules of grime.

    Behold:
bread batter slips from her hands, sugar skulls
buried underneath the bakery.

San Andreas does not hesitate. It will eat you alive.
Drag you from your hair
      sprinkle sand on your eyes
      crunch up your bones and spit them out
      you are not anew
you are just a nuisance

She will wonder one day, how did this happen?
She will think back to it
      to the bakery
      to the church
      to San Andreas.
She will whisper it
      Terremoto

Aventura

There are no mistakes in life, says Yolis.

    Only adventure

                                    aventura

the bus will get stuck on the road
on the way to Baños.

She will walk on the slippery roadside,
looking for a street vendor
to give her something sweet.

She giggles, soaking wet after a visit to El Pailón del Diablo
she gives us indigenous teas (sacrilege, screeches the priest)
and swaddles us in heavy wool blankets.

She dances in the too-tight aisle when a stranger
busks on the bus. We hide our faces, embarrassed
Deep inside, we know these are the memories
we will cherish.

Hiding underneath blankets on the truck bed,
feeling nauseous with her chaotic driving

She kisses us goodnight. Makes us pray.
We listen to her snores shake the house at night

When they ask me about adventure, I will talk about her.

I will talk about aventura.

Pastaza Te Lleva

Cuidado, allí va el río Pastaza
esa corriente—una fortaleza de movimiento y agua
El Pastaza, un corazón frío y furioso
Pastaza no muestra misericordia para nadie
dios maldado

en las tormentas, Pastaza se hincha
traga la tierra y piedra en un mordisco
baboso. Todos seremos víctimas de
Pastaza

un día, cuando la tierra
ya no puede aguantar más

aquí viene,
no hay tiempo para huir.
no resistas
Pastaza te lleva,
te lleva…

Tungurahua

Fiery tongue, spitting molten rock.
Shake the cities with your anger.

I am sorry, Tungurahua.
For your land has been uprooted in front of your
eyes.

They clog your rivers with their filth.
They kill your creatures with their bullets.
They drive your people away.

I hear your despairing roars.
I see your tears explode out of you
coating the city in ash.

Tungurahua, I wait for you.
I embrace you
when you can
no longer withstand your pain,
I will crown you Empress.
You will be free, at last.

Throat of fire
scream.

When My Abuelas Get Drunk

They giggle on the couch.
Long for their younger bodies, the ones that
could hold down their liquor better.

Yolis tells Chica about her crystal cheese platter.
Her husband's wedding gift.
The alcohol bottle breaks on the
kitchen counter,
but the cheese platter stays in pristine condition.
Chica asks her why she loves him, still.
Yolis points to the cheese platter.

Chica shakes her head, tipping her weight
side to side.
She takes a large gulp of her wine, hoping
that the sweetness of it will remove the bitter
aftertaste of loss in her mouth.

Chica mumbles
something about un pecado—
they remain silent.

They will hear him screeching soon
"Yolanda! Yolanda!"
Yolis will run to him, stumbling
to meet his needs.

Chica will scowl, acutely aware of their powerlessness.

The cheese platter will remain,
unbroken

Una Oda A Mi Mami Yolis

Como te quiero: la luchadora,
la señora que me enseña la
belleza de ser mujer

feminino divino,
Maria sagrada.
Toma el dulce vino,
que te ofrece
esta mano quebrada

Te van a dudar,
te dicen que no eres nada.
No saben la verdad.

Nunca dejes de luchar,
guerrera única.

Ángel

Chica calls me su amor, su ángel.
So I scald my back and sew pigeon feathers
underneath my shoulder blades.

Un ángel no llora
So I pick my skin raw and let the open wounds
absorb the salty tears

Un ángel debe ser feliz
So I find happiness in the little things—
In Chica's care, in her smile, in her laugh.

Do not be mistaken: I love the pain.
the suffering, ordained by a higher love—
a sacrifice I am willing to pay if

it means forever keeping her in my heart
so I pray: Virgen María, Padre nuestro
strengthen my shabby wings

I want to fly with her. Show her the world.
Give her the opportunities she never got.
Ease her pain.

Chica tells me that this isn't necessary
my existence is enough
it always has been

en tu alma vive mi esperanza / en tus manos está mi corazón / no te alejes que muero si no estás

You will be number one

prologue

She had dreams, too, once.
(she killed that animal a long time ago.
skinned it and hand-sewed the hide
into a pair of boots)
her blood-caked fingernails are forever stained.

i.

Say it, mijita: "Soy número uno"
I am number one
Taste the worn leather that Yolis works with.
Nostrils tingling with the stench of shoe polish
and a thick, viscous, waxy glue.
Remember, mijita: "Tu eres número uno"

ii.

Call it ambition,
desperation?
Papi knows best. Papi says that education
is the one-way ticket across the chasm
between us and them (your dear abuelíta and tías who cannot retire
and will die at their stations in el almacén while thinking about
shoes)

iii.

Go enroll in honors science courses,
because being the only Latina in the class
makes you stand out.
(later you can write your college essays on this,
pull some emotional bullshit about how you want to

be a pioneer for Latinas in STEM)
    why are pioneers praised
    but immigrants despised?

You tell them that you want to be A writer. An author. A poet.
Papi says that writing didn't pay the bills
Yolis's tears clean her face, leaving her cheeks glossy
like the shoes Papi cleaned for lunch money

                                                iv.
Chew through the shoe laces around your neck
You are hungry to fulfill Papi's and Yolis'
wishes (the laces only
get tighter)

Stop writing, then
You do.
A wounded animal. collapsed. Ribs crisscross its body
the same way you lace up the boots Yolis made for you

                                                v.
It screams, screeching your name
in the school hallway
don't look back.
That dream of writing must die with it.
Think of your Yolis, mijita.

                          epilogue
You think of her as you push the poison
into your neck, watching the animal writhe.
Staggering away from its stiff body
you smile,

Yolis' promise: fulfilled
Whatever it takes.
Lo que sea necesario.

Ave Maria

I sit down my Chica, my beautifully Catholic grandmother
in her tiny apartment.
I ask her about La Virgencita—the Virgin Mary.
I want to understand. So I listen
to "Ave Maria" on repeat.
> *(Et benedictus, Et benedictus fructus ventris.*
> *Ventris tui, Iesus. Ave Maria)*
> Barbra Streisand's interpretation
then the choral classic, followed by
the orchestral version.

I create a Virgen shrine in my room.
A delicate white statue sits on my dresser.
I blow off the dust demons
> *(If you invoke the blessed Virgin when you are tempted, she will*
> *come at once to your help, and Satan will leave her)*
she shall be pure.
> *(Behold, a virgin shall conceive)*
I put roses next to her shrine. Ones that my Chica picks from
the neighbors' rose bush.
She picks them so fast, not even the heavens
notice it.

I open up a playlist titled
Cantos a la Virgen de Guadalupe.
Surprised by how upbeat the music is—
synthy trumpets, an electronic keyboard

plays the backbone melody.
Children sing jolly lyrics,
>   *(Let us run to Mary, and, as her little children…)*
their innocence seeps into my ears.
They recount Her story,
Her glory goes hand in hand
with Mexican Pride but

my Chica isn't Mexican. She's Guatemalan.
My teacher tells me that La Virgen
is a product of colonialism,
a perfectly crafted Catholic lie.
>   *(Let us entrust to her intercession the daily prayer for peace,*
>   *especially in places where the senseless logic of violence is most*
>   *ferocious…)*
I wince at those words,
tinted glass nicks my hands, which were
folded in prayer to La Virgen.

Rainbow poncho, beaded and braided,
feels heavy on my back. Are the dried roses
my Chica puts next to her Virgen shrine
just old blood stains come to life?

My Chica calls my teacher un pendejo
Says it's a sin to suggest such a thing.
>   *(These all continued with one accord in prayer and*
>   *supplication.)*
She reminds me that it was, indeed,
an indigenous man who told the story of

La Virgen de Guadalupe.

I wonder if she knows that Juan Diego's original name was Cuauhtlatoatzin.

Dos:

Las mujeres mágicas también sufren

No take backs

there is an ocean between You and your country—crossed it a long time ago, treading water and swallowing seaweed and salt. you are a navigator (that's what you tell yourself. nobody believes it but you) a water wielder, a conqueror of the current. you know what happens to fish that fight it. you glide on seafoam and aquatic funnels until your fingers no longer shrivel in the water. your eyes stop stinging. the ocean boils. you are bleached, belly up like the coral you were told to destroy. long gone are the colors of the ocean.

don't think about it. don't panic because you don't remember how to find your way home. don't shudder as you suck away at everything and everything that reminds you of You. it's nice to float with the flow.

one day you forget how to breathe underwater. you flounder your way up to the surface. expecting land. expecting home. there is an ocean between You and your country. as you drown, you look up to the surface, hoping for You to come and take you home. You can't make it.

there is an ocean between You and your country.

First gen

Piano trills. Shoe tapping. Crying children,
god I can't stand the sound of crying children
Got daddy issues, no shit.
My grandfather trusts nobody,
so he controls them instead.
Believes that discipline will fix a broken kid. Calls it tough love.
Yeah, tough when all the grandkids are scared of him.

TV static. Tell them. Tell them. Tell him.
Somewhere behind that feminine,
submissive mask is a fierce lioness.
She will break every single bottle in the house.
Pour it all down their throat. Drown them in it.
The mask is stitched with diamond thread.
You stitched it yourself to protect them from Her.
Your time is running out. Death waits for nobody.
You must decide, my dear.
When will She be free?

Apple juice. Sugary milk. Oversalted rice.
This is normal.
The men say that a couple of shots of whiskey
will cure a cold. Don't believe them.
They're just alcoholics,
the whole lot of them.
The women say that garlic juice cures a sore throat. Natural antibiotics, they
say.

It's tough out here,
so the women brew Coke with cinnamon
and lemon on the old stove.
It cures fevers, they say.
Do not doubt them.
These home remedies will work.
They always will.

Chica doesn't smile in photos

she / does not / smile
                anymore / not in the photos /
                at least / she lost that smile a long time /
                ago / when her husband /
                my papa / died /
                she can only / conjure / a forced /
                grimace / if that /
                we do not / bother her /
                about it / anymore /
                we've accepted it / as her truth /
                her grief / his death /
                i think he /
                would want her /
                to smile /

"cuando papa se fue, mi sonrisa también se fue"
                                        -    Chica /

Chica's bedtime songs

Chica siempre nos cantaba canciones
En la cena: Los cochinitos que
roncan y roncan y vuelven a roncar

Cada niña con una canción tan individual como ella, llena
con un amor que solo los angelitos llevan

Cuando cierro los ojos, puedo ver el campo
de mis sueños. Las mariposas, volando
en el aire libre.
Allí están todos los animales,
Los pollítos que dicen *pio pio pio*
cuando tienen hambre
cuando tienen frío

Un día, el campo desaparecerá de mis sueños
como mi niñez.

Cuando los cielos
lucen con las estrellas.
Allí regresaré al campo, la voz de mi abuela
Será mi guía.

sabes bien, que volveré
mariposa, oh, mariposa
junto a ti, me quedaré

The lemon picking thief

My abuela is a thief.
In the broad daylight
she walks down my street, oversized jacket
clinging to her tiny frame

She disguises herself—
walking the dogs, the pitter-patter of their paws
synchronized to her step
A lemon tree of her stature stands
right at the intersection.

Commence the robbery
She pulls out a reusable shopping
bag from under her jacket.
Soundlessly tiptoeing to the tree with her
zapatos de viejíta, she snatches
one, two, three, four lemons
off the tree

holding her breath, the protesting
branches rattle.
Bag in one hand, leashes
in the other, she laughs

Now, she puts on her second disguise:
a grandma with groceries walking the dogs,
even they are oblivious to her crime.

As for us?
We get free lemons, for life.

Ana Dominga is dead

Picture it:
 a full voicemail inbox.
Hola, Ana Domingíta
 unopened letters.
Es Marti, solo quiero saber cómo estás
 skid marks on the street.
Llámame cuando puedas, porfis.
 bloodied broken glass
 squeezed metal, candy
 bones crunch under Collisions'
 Wrath.

Ana Dominga
who helped Chica with her papers
who cared for and loved
my mother and aunt
who still received letters from Chica,
hand-drawn hearts and butterflies in the spring,
baby Jesus and Christmas trees in the winter.
that Ana Dominga

 car crash in March
 Chica found out in May.
 she got eye surgery that day,
 a plastic patch over her eye
 to protect it? not from the sun
 but from her tears

from her nails
  (she claws at her smile lines and eye bags
  hoping it will take her back to when
  she was young with Ana Dominga)
Picture it:
  a family scrambling around the house
    Should we give Chica gabapentin?
  "Ay, Dios mío," repeated again and
  again in a tiny room. even the dogs
  come in to check on Chica
    Siéntate, *Chica*
  mother holds her tears back
  the granddaughters watch. one
  chokes on dinner as she cries.
    What do you mean, Chica missed the funeral?
  Father holds his head down.
  He cannot always be strong.

  Chica asked the family to track down
  Ana Dominga's family
  through Facebook.
  fruitless.

    Chica has not talked about Ana Dominga,
    nobody asks.
    everyone is too afraid to rekindle her pain.

  how can you miss your best friend's funeral?
    because they were countries apart.
    because families and friends fall out of

touch but Chica never

forgets. so she sends the voicemails
she sends letters with tiny drawings
springing butterflies and shivering saints.

Chica's morning prayers are longer, now
        Ana Dominga is memory.

here is how you miss your best friend's funeral
1. a collision. a body bag. smeared lipstick kisses the gravel
2. an expensive international phone call fee. an impoverished country.
3. a phone call, never made until the voicemails build up
4. a phone call, made months too late.

Picture it:
        two women who fought together,
        laughed together. fire and fire, a roaring spirit.
        a life blown out, a dead silence.
        suddenly:
                "Ana Dominga is dead."

Yolis, did you know?

when your son left you
at seventeen years old.
did you know he would survive?

did you know that he
crossed the border, terrified and
alone?

did you know that he would make it?
eighteen units each semester with a full-time job,
commute hours each day to work at a bank
in Pasadena

do you know that the woman who
got him his papers, years after he
became a naturalized citizen,
was discovered by the FBI and imprisoned?

do you know how much he misses you?
how, he watches all the whatsapp videos
you send him

because, it reminds him of you
you: Yolis, the woman who sent her oldest
to an unknown country
on prayers and tears
the woman who braved the

uncertainty because she believed

Yolis, you didn't know
but you believed.

Sana sana

Cuando tienes gripe
tú tienes un remedio:
coca cola hervida con canela y
miel de abeja para la fiebre
      jugo de limón para un picado
      Pitahaya y té de manzanilla
      para un dolor de panza.

          puedes llenarme con todas las yerbas
          y bebidas hervidas que tienes.
          pero nunca encontrarás un remedio
          para este corazón herido.

          el mar nos separa
          las corrientes llevan mi dolor
          hasta las profundidades
          allí me pudro
          carne se congela
          mis dientes se llenan de
          algas

          yo te arrastro a las profundidades
          los dos debemos sufrir.
          maridos, somos
          un par de pecadores unidos
          con una cadena de vidrio
          envuelto por nuestra

cintura.

en la cocina, tú siempre trabajas
buscas un remedio para los dos.
y sé que nunca lo encontrarás
porque yo lo escondí hace mucho

tiempo, como pasa el tiempo aquí
en la obscuridad.
no hay nada más que hacer
solo sufrir

y tú?
cada día cantando
          sana sana…

My Mami Yolis the free woman

My Mami Yolis is
the woman who sent her oldest
to the unknown on prayers and pocket change.

She's fierce, claims she's independent but
I know that when my grandfather hollers
at her, she will
bend to him. She will bring him
breakfast.

Sweet and servile, she will plate his meal
just to his liking. She will
bring him a fork when he asks for it.
Fill up his glass of water. Serve him seconds.

I watch and wonder
how a woman with so much ambition
and drive.
Could sputter and stop, putting
it all to a halt. Do it so willingly,
so effortlessly.

My Mami Yolis tells me
to be number one.
I cry for her because she refuses
to cry for herself.

She could've been number one.
She could've done so much.
In America, dreams come true. In America,
number one becomes a possibility.
But she stayed back:
for the kids
for the factory
for my grandfather

She says she is free. I don't believe it.
I think she's conditioned herself
to settle. She pierced her
eyes, blinded herself for life
a long time ago.

How can a woman be simultaneously
so strong and so trapped?

I want to sever the lacy chains around
her limbs with shards of fine china.
I want to gently hand-sew eyes back
into empty sockets.

In my dreams, Mami Yolis is free.
She is wild, untamed.
She whispers stories of her youth
in my ear. Stories about the horses
she used to take care of. Her eyes
no longer glimmer
with a desire to be like them.

The stallions gallop into the sunset
Mami Yolis joins them.
I cry happy tears.
There is broken china and torn lace
all around me. I leave it there. For him,
of course.

I know, somewhere far away from me, from him
from everything that
ever held her back,
Mami Yolis is giggling
She's free.

Good girl

Say buenos días and buenas noches to mami and papi
Be wary of ese tío borracho, he will slap your ass when he's feeling macho
Don't let those breasts sag. Men want tetas de muñeca, not una lechera
Niña bonita, why you so fría?
Shave down all your hair, and don't forget to share (*quiero comerte enterita*)

Remember: tú eres una niña. You are a girl.
Weak, meek, with silky sleek sheets that you will wash once the world is done with you
You will smile as everyone leaves.
Rebellion tastes sweet, but not as sweet as you

Siéntate
Spread your legs wide open for them.
(this is what you were born to do.
this is what good girls do)

Eres una niña todavía, posing in the bathtub for
strangers. Strip slowly, elongate your waist,
menea ese culíto, grab your b-cup breasts
(you are a child, after all)
this is routine now.

The women in the telenovelas you watch

have big breasts and tiny waists. They wear
bodycon dresses and heels. You want a boob job.
And a tummy tuck.
Maybe that would make you better.

You sleep naked at night. Free real estate, they say.
They call you all sorts of things. But good girl
is your favorite.
All your life, you've been told to follow the rules
You do not question it anymore.

So when they come for you
actually, come for you.
You do not fight. You do not run.
You become the only thing they wanted you to be.
A good girl.

Manuela Monzón de Mendoza, the poet

Chica tells me that
her mother was a poet
                    she had it all:
                    the dead husband
                    the alcohol addiction
                    the insanity
        what is my talent then?
        generational gift?
        generational curse?
                    when I was little,
                    Chica would tell me stories
                    of her mother—
                    the beatings
                    how grief grabbed her by the neck—
                    stuffed her into
                    a bottle,
and dragged her away
until she couldn't handle her
existence.
                    I am eerily similar to
                    Manuela Monzón de Mendoza.
                    the insanity,
                    the fragile balance between
                    tolerating existence and
                    tormenting myself to death
so I google search: *how do you break generational patterns*

it seems as if nobody has the answer.

Manuela Monzón de Mendoza
you are the shadow I cannot shake off
you are part of me, through history.
I will never be able to escape
you, but god, oh god
I will certainly try

NOTES

Terremoto

    On February 4, 1976, a 7.5-magnitude earthquake struck Guatemala. Chica lived through the horrors of that earthquake along with my mom, my aunt, and my grandfather. All of the descriptions in the poem are personal anecdotes I have from Chica. The 1976 earthquake killed 23,000 people and destroyed entire neighborhoods, including the one where Chica lived.

Aventura

    Aventura is based on real places in Ecuador. Baños is a province in Ecuador that is known for its thermal, volcanic baths. Not only that, but Baños is full of tourist spots, such as waterfalls, rainforests, and rivers. El Pailón del Diablo is one of the waterfalls I had the privilege of visiting. Also known as the Devil's Cauldron, this waterfall is known for its violent, rushing waterfalls. The locals say that if you look closely, you can see the face of the devil within the rock of the waterfall.

Pastaza te lleva

    El Río Pastaza runs through a city known as Puyo in the Pastaza province of Ecuador. The river is known for being violent and destructive. The locals warn their children to avoid it because those who fall into its waters do not come out alive. I chose to write this poem entirely in Spanish because I felt it was the only way I could capture the true magnificence of this river. I will not provide translations for this poem because the English words do not do this river justice.

Tungurahua

Tungurahua is a volcano in the province of Tungurahua. It is a popular tourist attraction and the only volcano I have seen erupt. Tungurahua means "throat of fire." As Ecuador invests more in tourism and in oil as means of national income, more and more of its wildlife is getting destroyed. Please consider donating to The Rainforest Trust to help save Ecuador's beautiful rainforests from getting destroyed.

Una oda a mi Mami Yolis

This is another poem written fully in Spanish. It was written specifically for Mami Yolis to understand, so I will not provide a translation for this poem. I think there is power in not providing translation and being unapologetic in my use of Spanish. I think Mami Yolis would appreciate this.

Ave Maria

Though it is easy to think that I am dismissing La Virgen Maria with this poem, that is simply not the case. I love La Virgen Maria. I have a small statue of her in my room. However, I believe it is important to reconcile with the truth behind the Spanish conquest of Mexico and the effects of it. Forced assimilation was deadly in Mexico. Entire civilizations were completely wiped out from history. Ave Maria begs the reader to question their beliefs, without utterly disrespecting them.

First gen

I listened to "United In Grief" by Kendrick Lamar over and over again while writing this poem.

Chica doesn't smile in photos

This poem is dedicated to my grandfather, Alfredo, who passed away from cancer in 2008. I love you forever and always, Papa.

Ana Dominga is dead

To Ana Dominga, whom I never met. Thank you for being such a beautiful friend to Chica. Thank you for showing her what true friendship is. May you rest in peace.

Acknowledgments

First and foremost, I need to thank my beautiful abuelas, Chica and Mami Yolis. This chapbook would not be here without them. Thank you, Yolis, for always putting a smile on my face and for teaching me how to cherish the unpredictability of life. Thank you, Chica, for always supporting my dream of writing.

Thank you to the editors at Somos En Escrito: Jenny, Scott, Armando, Luz, for taking on this chapbook with me. I am honored to be debuting my work with Somos En Escrito,

My family: Mom, Dad, Dani, and Sofi, thank you for your endless support in my writing journey. Mom and Dad, thank you for constantly engaging with me and my poetry. I appreciate it more than you can imagine.

Thank you to all my friends, my CSSSA buddies, the poetry gang, and everyone else who has supported me in my poetry journey. You all constantly cheered me on and reminded me of my value, even when I could not see it myself. I would not be here without all the love and happiness you guys bring me daily.

To my teachers and professors, Mrs. Poffenbarger, Mr. Welch, Professor Crotwell, Professor Williams, and Profe Ochoa…the biggest thank you to you all. Thanks for playing such an important role in getting me to where I am today.

So many people allowed me to get to where I am today. I would not be here without every single one of them. Thank you to everyone who cheered me on, prayed for me, and believed in me. You all give me the strength to keep on going. Thank you.

ABOUT THE AUTHOR

Isabella Santana is a 19-year old poet from Los Angeles, California. She is the proud daughter of Ecuadorian and Guatemalan immigrants. She is part of the new generation of Latine authors and works to amplify Latine voices wherever she goes. She has received recognition from Urban Word as a Los Angeles Youth Poet Ambassador in 2022 and 2023. She has performed her poetry for organizations such as Univision. She is the author of Abuela Lore (2024, Somos en escrito Literary Foundation Press), her debut chapbook. Connect with her on IG @Bellaassantana

SOMOS EN ESCRITO

DEDICATED TO PUBLISHING
RAZA AUTHORS

Somos en escrito Literary Foundation Press is an all Raza-run publishing house based in Berkeley, California, dedicated to promoting Raza writers who express the diverse narratives of our communities. We record Raza realities and histories en escrito to inspire solutions through storytelling, rather than provide mere visibility. Our books aim to break oppressive cycles and call others to action towards a future where our gente not only exist, but thrive.

Join our Literary Lucha!

Other books by
SOMOS EN ESCRITO
LITERARY FOUNDATION PRESS

Somos Xicanas
Edited by Luz Schweig, Armando Rendón,
Jenny Irizary and Scott Russell Duncan (2024)

Our Creative Realidades: A Nonfiction Anthology
Edited by Armando B. Rendón, Scott Russell Duncan,
Jenny Irizary and Luz Schweig (2024)

Corazón de agua/Heart of Water
by Xánath Caraza
Translated by Sandra Kingery (2024)

Chicanofuturism Now! Visions of a Raza Future
Edited by Scott Russell Duncan, Armando B. Rendón
and Jenny Irizary (2024)

Bella: Collector of Cuentos
By Carmen Baca (2022)

El Porvenir, ¡Ya! Citlalzazanilli Mexicatl:
A Chicano Science Fiction Anthology
Edited by Scott Russell Duncan, Armando B. Rendón
and Jenny Irizary (2022)

Our Grandfathers were Braceros and We Too
by Abel Astorga Morales and Rosa Marta Zárate Macías (2021)

Chicano Manifesto (50th Anniversary Edition)
by Armando B. Rendón, (2021)

Death Song of the Dragón Chicxulub
by R. CH. Garcia (2021)

Undesirable—Race and Remembrance:
New & Selected Poems
by Robert René Galván (2020)

Insurgent Aztlán
The Liberating Power of Cultural Resistance
by Ernesto Todd Mireles (2020)

Theorizing César Chávez:
New Ways of Knowing STEM
by Armando A. Arias (2020)

Postcards from a PostMexican
by Álvaro Ramírez (2020)

Made in the USA
Las Vegas, NV
03 April 2024